THERE'S ONLY ONE OF ME HERE TODAY

by

SANDRA M. BRUNSMANN

THERE'S ONLY ONE OF ME HERE TODAY

For information write to: S. M. Brunsmann
1462 Royal Springs Drive
St. Louis, Missouri 63122-7134 (USA)

First Edition
ISBN: 0-9632178-0-1

Library of Congress Catalog Card Number: 92-90249

Designed and typeset by:
K-A-V Publishing Company
(a division of)
Ancona & Associates, Inc.
(314) 394-2019

Printed in the United States of America

*****

This book is dedicated to the women in our lives;
may they have the courage to take action and
solve their dilemma of anger ... at home ... in the
workplace ... with money ... and with men.

Every Good Wish!

Sandra Brunsmann

Special Thanks:

to ...

Darlene Fellhauer, Sue Hobart, Pam Anderson, Janet Lewis, Pat Clancy, Cathy Jones, Laraine Reed ... my friends; a special couple, Bud and Louise Thackeray ... and my sister, Jill Lauman.

They have been an inspiration to me over the years. Their friendship and encouragement helped me write this book. Also, to the many clients and the women in the audiences of my workshops who have shared their experiences with the dilemma of anger ... at home ... in the workplace ... with money ... and with men,

to ...

My parents, Ruth Josephine (nee Byrne) and Albert Henry Spaeth (Speth).

to ...

My husband Tom, who helped me to see life with a sense of humor.

to ...

The 1990 Virginia Slims Opinion Poll conducted by the Roper Organization was a valuable resource to me; and thanks to them for allowing me to use it.

to ...

Carlene Rowley with Royal Banks of Missouri.

This book title was settled after I impatiently honked for the drive-up bank teller. She came to my service with a smile and said very politely, *"There's only one of me here today."*

to ...

Elaine Viets, who encouraged me to get an editor.

Every Good Wish!

Sandra Brunsmann

CONTENTS

... continued

PREFACE

Women do not have to be coaxed into changing the things in their lives that are making them unhappy or abused. They want the peace they deserve as human beings. What happens in our English Speaking Culture is a Period of Unpleasantness that is impossible to work through for many women. It is what people do to you with words, body language, tone of voice, money, etc., to keep you from changing your life style.

Sometimes the Period of Unpleasantness leads to physical harm. Nearly all instances of physical abuse starts with verbal abuse. What do these women do with their anger? Here is the dilemma they face ... at home ... in the workplace ... with money ... with men.

The purpose of this book is to convert this anger and put a plan into action, so they can get past the anger stage. Anger takes too much energy. When it is turned inward, it leads to depression.

Therefore, it is not a surprise that more women are depressed than men. "Women's risk for depression exceeds that of men by two to one." This was discovered by the American Psychological Association Task Force on Women and Depression between 1987 and 1989. The Task Force identified the following contributors to women's greater risk for depression; "family roles and intimate relationships, work roles, victimization and poverty."

The National Women's Health Network states that depression is "especially prevalent among women. Some factors associated with depression include a lack of control in one's job or life (homemakers with small children are particularly susceptible), ... and the experience of stressful life events." Women ask for help early on when they have a dilemma with anger. Frequently they ask doctors and other professionals to help them. Doctors put them on tranquilizers and shut them up. Professional counselors *listen* to them for a fee. Of the twenty-six prevalent chronic conditions reported between 1980 and 1988 by the U.S. National Center for Health Statistics, <u>Vital and Health Statistics</u>, twenty-two were experienced more by females than males.

The Virginia Slims Survey of 1990 compared their survey of women in 1970 and the results showed that women were angrier than they have ever been ... at home ... in the workplace ... with money ... with men. Doctors and professional *listeners* are not working for these women because they are not learning to develop their individual action plan to deal with their anger. The recent Thomas-Hill hearings and Smith- trial illustrated very clearly that a woman is not heard on her own word, but a man is "categorically" heard.

Please contact me personally if you have any questions about the suggested action plans offered in the chapters.

Every Good Wish!

Sandra Brunsmann

HOW IT WORKS ...

... how to use this book

The main reason for writing this book was to give you an action plan to solve the dilemma of anger for women ... at home ... in the workplace ... with money ... with men.

The chapters are set up as separate plans so that you can read the ones that apply to your life. Chapters are easy to access so they can be applied to enhance your action plan. For instance, the chapter on the <u>Period of Unpleasantness</u> and <u>Same 24 Hours</u>, are useful in dealing with personal excuses like, "but if you had my family ... if you had my boss ... if you had my salary ... if you had my man."

The <u>Women's Movement</u> chapter is important so you can see the importance of supporting and mentoring other women so that collectively we can be powerful. When 53 percent of a society are women, 53 percent should be heard.

At the end of each chapter is an outline for you to complete to get you started on your plan. It is designed to move you to action and set a date to begin the plan. It is designed to enable you to discover the personal sabotage that you are choosing to stay angry. It is designed to show you what to do differently to get you past the Period of Unpleasantness. It is designed to guide you to better time management. It is designed to allow you to measure your progress. It is designed to solve the dilemma of anger ... in the home ... in the workplace ... with money ... with men. A simple example follows.

Why did you read this chapter? *(I can't do all the housework)*

_____

_____

What is your resistance to the suggestions for change?

(I don't want family members to be angry with me)

_____

_____

What techniques have you chosen to initiate the change?

(I will decide the chores I will do)

_____

_____

When are you going to start? __*(6-17-92)*__

Every Good Wish!

Sandra Brunsmann

Chapter 1

DOUBLE JEOPARDY

"I realized a long time ago that a belief which does not spring from a conviction in the emotions is no belief at all."
                                                                    -Evelyn Scott

Women and the dilemma of anger: It's time for women to re-examine values and ideals. American values and ideologies are in conflict with the emergence of women into the working world. This has reshaped the nature of the workplace and family; and raised issues of childcare, eldercare, and leadership to the forefront of our social consciences.

According to the 1990 Virginia Slims Opinion Poll conducted by the Roper Organization, 77 percent of women favor efforts to improve the status of women. Men's views have changed, and today we find 74 percent of men favor efforts to improve women's status. While there have been tremendous changes in male attitudes toward women in society—particularly in terms of the growing majority of men who favor efforts to "strengthen women's stature—" changes in their behavior have been slower to materialize. Today, 55 percent of women say women are looked upon with more respect than they were ten years ago. A majority of women and men are optimistic about women's status in the future.

Anger exists when particular conditions are not met. Author Nancy Friday said, "society would rather we always wore a pretty face, women have been trained to cut off anger." Anger can bring us to action but we need to have a plan. When no action is taken, and the resentments are held, our anger turns inward, and negatively influences and complicates our lives.

Because we are uncomfortable with anger, it becomes more powerful. When we go to work angry and resentful because of home issues, it affects our careers.

This book has been written to get women past the anger, past the awareness of anger, past blaming others for the lifestyles they are living. It is written as an action plan to get women to be in charge of their lives and to be in relationships because they choose to be there. Too many women feel stuck in their relationships.

The chapters are written on separate issues. Each chapter is designed to stimulate an awareness of the issue. Suggestions are offered so you can take the information pertinent to your situation and develop your own game plan and associated time table. Then the issue can be resolved to your satisfaction and you can be in charge of that part of your life.

The concept of being in charge of your life means that you have resolved issues to the point where you can go on with your life and not be using energy on anger and resentment. It's like being in a "gerbil cage," which means that you are going around in circles, saying you want changes, but not having the courage to develop the game plan to stop the wheel from turning. Once you take action, you can open the door and set yourself free to get on with life.

*****

Why did you read this chapter? (See: "How it Works - how to use this book")

_____

_____

_____

What is your resistance to the suggestions for re-examining values and ideals?

_____

_____

_____

What values and ideals have you chosen to change?

_____

_____

_____

When are you going to start? _____

Chapter 2

WHAT DO YOU WANT?

"If I'd known this is what it would be like to have it all, I might have been willing to settle for less."
                                                    -Lily Tomlin

*P*ersonal life, do you want one? What do you want? Asked to rate how satisfied they are with aspects of their own lives, the overwhelming majority of women in the 1990 Virginia Slims Opinion Poll continue to find their greatest satisfactions in their most intimate relationships with friends, lovers, husbands and children. The bottom end of the satisfaction scale relates to jobs and finances. At the same time, the 1990 Poll also indicates that women are angrier at men today than they were twenty years ago.

It is true that since the mid-1970s, a majority of women have said that the ideal life combines marriage, career and children. The preference for this kind of life, which increased from 1974 to 1985, has since suffered a noticeable, if modest, decline. The proportion of women saying that they personally would prefer to combine marriage, career and children declined six points to 57 percent since 1985. The proportion of women who would choose a dual-earner, shared-responsibility marriage dropped from 57 percent in 1985 to 53 percent in 1990.

In part, this shift reflects the difficulties women have experienced in trying to balance work, marriage and children. Since most women work out of a perceived financial need, they are unlikely to retreat from the workplace in large numbers. But many women are re-examining the balance of work, marriage and children.

As the institutions of society adapt to accommodate their needs, women will reduce the pressure on themselves to be super women.

What needs to change in order to reduce that super women image and bring balance of personal, family and career?

Try the exercise below to find out what will work for you.

List the people in your life: Personal/Family/Career

Indicate a **Y** if you are spending the time with them that you would like. Indicate a **N** if you are not spending the time with them that you would like. If you answer with a N, write the reason for the lack of time. Write what you can do to change the reason for your excuse.

example:

(daughter)   (N)   (too tired)   (prioritize time)

(friend Mary) (N)   (not enough time)   (call & set date)

Paradise Awaits You

FIRST-CLASS MAIL
ZIP + 4 BARCODED
U.S. POSTAGE PAID
FT. MYERS, FL
PERMIT NO. 69

Pin #033007034

Sky International - Largo
13191 Starkey Rd North St 5
Largo, FL 34643

Dear CAROL,

You have been selected for a
9 day Florida/Caribbean Vacation
Package, including all accommodations,
a round trip cruise, and much more.
Call us 1-800-759-5052, Ext. 430B
Mon-Fri 10 am to 10 pm EST,
Sat. 10 am to 4 pm EST,
If busy keep calling!
Sincerely,

Laura Smith
Vacation Coordinator

CAROL BEAR
108 FENWICK DR -
FERGUSON MO 63135-2823

NAME	Y/N	CAUSE	CHANGE
____	__	_____	_____
____	__	_____	_____
____	__	_____	_____
____	__	_____	_____
____	__	_____	_____
____	__	_____	_____
____	__	_____	_____
____	__	_____	_____
____	__	_____	_____
____	__	_____	_____

After you identify the imbalances in your life between personal, family and career, look for the ways that you can balance the three. It will not happen by wishful thinking, blaming others or denying it exists.

Balance in your personal life will happen when you decide your happiness and good health are important.

Figuring out how we want to spend our days and taking charge of how we live each twenty-four hours is the way we can get happy and productive. It can't be someone else's plan for us. It can't be someone else's plan for how the house looks and what you need to do to keep it that way. It can't be someone else's idea of what a perfect mother should be doing and therefore what you should be doing. It can't be someone else's plan for where your career is heading and the time frame for realizing the plan. It can't be someone else's plan for how many friends you have and when you can see them. It can't be someone else's plan for how your relationship with your husband should be and what you should accept as "better or worse." (See Chapter 7, Same 24 Hours)

Look at each of the relationships and make decisions about the importance of the relationship. It is realistic that you would want to spend time with your immediate family and you can decide what amount of time and energy is possible for you at this time. This is not a permanent decision because your lifestyle will change and with a base decision you can re-evaluate the relationship easily.

When we are dealing with other people the next step is to determine what amount of energy and time they are willing to contribute to the relationship. This will take conversation and sharing of your feelings about the importance of the relationship. Remember, this is your project and it's not likely the rest of your world will be as enthused as you are about changing your life so that you are more comfortable. Change is very threatening to many people. Even in the best of circumstances, people will react in peculiar and non-loving ways. (See Chapter 11, Periods of Unpleasantness) The chart on the next page has been designed for you to better determine your needs.

GOALS   TARGET DATES FOR ACTION

Child   _____

Child   _____

Child   _____

Marriage   _____

Relationship   _____

Career   _____

Friends   _____

Education   _____

Caregiving   _____

Church   _____

Community   _____

Hobbies   _____

Empty Nest   _____

Retirement   _____

Other   _____

*****

Why did you read this chapter?

_____

_____

_____

What is your resistance to the suggestions for change?

_____

_____

_____

What techniques have you chosen to initiate change?

_____

_____

_____

_____

When are you going to start? _____

Chapter 3

STRESS

*"If I have to, I can do anything. I am strong, I am invincible,
I am woman."*

-Helen Reddy 1972

Stress is a greater fact of life for women today than at any other time since 1970. More women now than in 1985 believe that something is inevitably sacrificed when women work - and it is children whom they see suffering the most. In 1985, 21 percent of women were confident that nothing is neglected when women with families work. In 1990, just 14 percent would say this. Of women with children who work full-time, 61 percent say the conflicting demands of family and job put them under stress; and 56 percent say they feel guilty that they don't spend more time with their families. Another stress factor cited was "trying to live up to other people's expectations." Results showed 46 percent highest among 18-29 year olds, singles and those with children under 18 years of age.

Stress and how women cope with it: According to a Virginia Slims Opinion Poll, stress seems to be a way of life for most women today. Fifty-six percent say they have a good deal or fair amount of tension or stress in their lives, while 42 percent say they have very little or none. Men report somewhat less stress; 51 percent say they live under a good deal or fair amount of stress.

Subgroups of women reporting the highest levels of stress:

Women in executive or professional positions: (71 percent say they have a good deal or fair amount of stress in their lives, versus 60 percent of men in comparable positions);

Those who are separated or divorced (69 percent);

Women with children under 18 at home (66 percent);

Women in their thirties (66 percent); and 64 percent of women who work full-time versus 59 percent of women who work full-time and have children under 18, say they experience a good deal or fair amount of stress.

What causes stress in women's lives?: The two major culprits, according to the poll, are shortages of money (which 70 percent say is either a major or minor cause of stress in their lives; [See chapter 15, Mainly Money] and self-imposed pressure, 68 percent).

A majority of women also cite their children as a cause of stress (for 53 percent of all women with children and for 64 percent of women with children under 18). Interestingly, mothers who do not work outside the home report stress from their children to the same extent as all women. However, 50 percent of all women, 66 percent of women with children under 18 and 73 percent of employed women with children under 18 cite the amount of work they have to get done in the day as a source of stress.

How do women relieve stress at the end of the day?

At the top of the list is watching TV (77 percent often or sometimes do this to relieve stress); and listening to music (74 percent), followed by taking a bath/shower (68 percent), listening to the radio (67 percent), reading (66 percent) and talking on the telephone (66 percent).

Cited by between half and two-thirds of women, are shopping (60 percent), going for a walk (58 percent), cooking (54 percent) and taking a nap (53 percent). Between a quarter and a half of women say they work on a hobby to relieve stress (43 percent), exercise (37 percent), or play a game (27 percent).

Less popular antidotes for stress include a cocktail at home (22 percent), going out to a bar (12 percent), having a manicure or pedicure (10 percent), having a massage (9 percent), going to a spa (8 percent), and taking a tranquilizer (7 percent).

Despite the much-publicized health benefits of active exercise, including its value as a tension reliever, most Americans, women and men alike, appear to prefer sedentary activities as their main antidotes to stress.

To develop a new awareness of your stress reality, identify the cause of stress in your life.

Stressor	Cause	Excuse
(Boss)	*(Sexual Remarks)*	*(Afraid of being fired)*
_____	_____	_____
_____	_____	_____
_____	_____	_____
_____	_____	_____
_____	_____	_____
_____	_____	_____
_____	_____	_____
_____	_____	_____

Review your stressors and put them in priority order by numbering. Look closely at the stresses in relation to family, career and personal needs. Now you can develop a plan of action to take charge of your life and balance career, family and personal needs.

Stress has become a way of life for women in 1990 as they struggle to balance their roles of worker, mother, daughter, daughter-in-law and spouse. More working women than men say that they experience stress, 63 percent vs. 56 percent. The most conflicting is the role of work and family. Clearly something has got to give. The question is, what will it be? Why do some people react to stress with illness or death and others recover and go on and continue to lead productive lives. Suzette Haden-Elgin states in her latest book <u>Staying Well with the Gentle Art of Verbal Self-Defense</u> that researchers (Suzanne Koubasa, Salvatore Maddi and Aaron Antonovsky) have identified four crucial elements that go together and interact to create what they call hardiness. Hardy people not only can encounter stress without being harmed by it, they are often able to benefit from it. Here are the Four Cs that define hardiness.

COMMITMENT: The willingness to involve yourself in what you do. Being interested in events and eager to take part in them. Being interested in doing rather than in just passively observing life as it goes by.

CONTROL: The feeling that even when things are not going well, you still are not a helpless victim. The conviction that there are things you can do, choices you can make, steps you can take on your own behalf.

CHALLENGE: The ability to perceive a stressful event as an opportunity. The ability to look upon change as something potentially good and valuable, and the willingness to seek out that side of change instead of the down side. The ability to re-interpret events instead of being locked into just one perception of them.

COHERENCE: The ability to perceive the world and the demands the world makes upon you, as making sense-as a rational whole, rather than unrelated pieces "in loose formation.''

We know that stress itself is not the crucial factor in health, but that our reaction to the stress is what really matters. People with low hardiness are twice as likely to experience illness and accidents.

The thing that all four hardiness elements have in common is information. "You can't be committed to the unknown. You can't feel in control if you have no idea what's going to happen, or when or why. You can't perceive a stressful event as a challenge, if you don't know what it is or what it means. You can't make sense of your world in an informational void." Sojourner Truth, lecturer for women's rights, said "It is the mind that makes the body."

How can we measure this anger and resentment? Is it the suggested increase in child abuse, battered women and power ploys being experienced between the relationships of men and women? Nancy Friday, noted author, says, "Because society would rather we always wore a pretty face, women have been trained to cut off anger." We can get free of our anger if we choose to take appropriate action. Anger can be a healthy promoter of action. But when no action is taken, anger turns inward, negatively influencing our perceptions of all experiences. Because we are less at home with anger, it is more powerful. It surfaces in unrelated circumstances, complicating our lives in unnecessary and destructive ways.

Has rape increased since 1970? Yes. According to the U.S. Federal Bureau Investigation (FBI), Population-at-Risk-Rates and Selected Crime Indicators, annual Forcible rape has escalated from 37,990 in 1970 to 94,500 in 1989.

Women need to respond to this increased rate of rape and threat of physical violation.

*****

Why did you read this chapter?

_____

_____

_____

What is your resistance to the suggestions for change?

_____

_____

_____

What techniques have you chosen to initiate change?

_____

_____

_____

When are you going to start? _____

Chapter 4

SICK AND TIRED

"Pity is the deadliest feeling that can be offered to a woman."
-Vicki Baum

When do you get sick? Why is this relevant to being in charge of your life? Ask yourself the following questions.

When do you get sick? _____ *(Holidays)* _____

What constitutes sick for you? (headache, fever, cramps, PMS, stomach upset, back problems, bowel problems, neck and shoulder problems, insomnia, depression, sore throat, cough, sinus problems, gall bladder attack, indigestion, constipation, esophagitis, earache etc....)

How many times were you sick in the <u>last year</u>? _____

Name each sickness.

_____

What event precipitated the sickness?

_____

Who was involved?

_____

When did you first recognize the symptom?

_____

What did you do about it?

_____

Did you call a physician?

_____

Did you visit a physician?

_____

What was the diagnosis?

_____

Were others called into the treatment plan?

_____

Were you clear on your symptoms? _____ or, did you turn it over to the physician?

_____

How did each family member treat you during the sick period?

_____

How did your friend treat you during the sick period?

_____

How did your spouse treat you during the sick period?

_____

How did your workplace treat you during the sick period?

_____

What was the worst thing about being sick?

_____

What was the good thing about being sick?

_____

How many times have you been sick <u>this</u> year? _____

.

Name each sickness.

_____

What event precipitated the sickness?

_____

Who was involved?

_____

When did you first recognize the symptom(s)?

_____

What did you do about it?

_____

Did you call a physician?

_____

Did you visit a physician?

_____

What was the diagnosis?

_____

Were others called into the treatment plan?

_____

Were you clear on your symptoms? _____ or did you turn it over to the physician?

_____

How did each family member treat you during the sick period?

_____

How did your friends treat you during the sick period?

_____

How did your spouse treat you during the sick period?

_____

How did the workplace treat you during the sick period?

_____

What was the worst thing about being sick?

_____

What was the good thing about being sick?

_____

Evaluate last year's sick periods and this year's sick periods and see if you see any patterns regarding:

Type of sickness ____people involved _____

Family treatment ____spouse treatment _____

Workplace _____friends _____

Worst thing _____good thing _____

Times last year _____times this year _____

What is the most surprising thing you have learned from this evaluation?

_____

_____

What did you already know about your sick behavior?

_____

_____

What techniques do you have in place to increase your wellness potential?

_____

_____

Why have you ignored the connection between stress and illness in your life?

_____

How is sickness dealt with by your mother?

_____

How is sickness dealt with by your grandmother?

_____

How is sickness dealt with by your friends?

_____

How is sickness dealt with by your children?

_____

How is sickness dealt with by your mentor?

_____

How is sickness dealt with by your spouse?

_____

What happened when you were a child and you were sick?

_____

It is important to finish this exercise so you can decide the wellness game plan you will use for yourself. Be aware of the excuses you use to not take care of yourself. Be aware of the pattern of sickness you are choosing in your life. Be aware of the contradictions.

Author, Kathleen Casey Theisen said, "Pain is inevitable. Suffering is optional." Develop your personal game plan to deal with your pain.

*****

Why did you read this chapter?

_____

_____

What is your resistance to the suggestions for change?

_____

_____

What techniques have you chosen to initiate the change?

_____

_____

When are you going to start? _____

Chapter 5

CHILDREN'S HELP

"Most kids hear what you say; some kids do what you say; but all kids do what you do."

-Kathleen Casey Theisen

According to the Virginia Slims' report of 1990, equal numbers of men and women (32 percent) say that it would make a difference if the kids helped out with the household chores. How are you going to get your children to help?

Call a family meeting and give copies of the chores you are currently willing to do. Then provide copies of the remaining chores. This can be handled room by room and divided by daily, weekly, entertaining, spring cleaning, etc. (See Chapter 6, Chores)

Let the family discuss this new development. Remember you are through talking about it. The discussion should revolve now on what *they* are going to do to help. The more organized your sheets of chores are, the easier your children will be able to make decisions. Provide pencils and scrap paper for them to figure out how much time it will take to do the chores. Don't allow them to: draw you into discussions of why this is happening; make promises of future help or of how everybody else's mom/wife seems to manage; or ask why can't you offer bribes of some sort. Remember, you are through talking, now it is their turn.

Have a script rehearsed so that you can repeat the same message throughout this initial presentation of chores. It can go like this: "I am through talking about getting help around this house, I am showing you the chores I will be doing in the future, I am confident you will be able to work out the rest of the chores among yourselves."

Knowing the history of family discussions in your home will prompt you to think out where the family meeting should be. If there is a history of interruptions, screaming and hollering, etc., then a meeting at Dennys' Restaurant will do nicely. Why Dennys? It is a restaurant open 24 hours and is receptive to conversations after dinner. More importantly, it is a place where it would be socially unacceptable to loud talk and to pushing chairs away from the table.

After your announcement at the family meeting, be prepared for the family members to come to you individually and ask, "Why are you doing this to us?". If their statements begin with the following, "If you REALLY loved us ..." or "EVen YOU should ..." or "WHY don't you EVer ..." or "EVeryone underSTANDS why you ..." or "SOME mothers/wives would ..." or "DON'T you EVEN CARE ..."or similar statements; you don't need to answer because these questions are not questions in the usual sense. They are verbal abuse and you don't need to take the bait. (Suzette Haden-Elgin)

The family will have a number of options of how to respond to your latest effort of getting help around the house. Be prepared for at least two weeks of unpleasantness. This is most often difficult for women because we like to keep people happy and satisfied and have been socialized to be responsible for their comfort. (See Chapter 11, Period of Unpleasantness)

The worst case scenario will be to ignore you completely and let all the chores go unattended. They might begin to make verbally abusive attacks and try to make you feel guilty that you are not taking care of them like they think you should. They might bring friends home and try to shame you with the old, "DON'T you EVEN CARE what the neighbors think?" They might not speak to you or give you hugs or phone messages. Remember, you have talked about getting help before and it will take a while before they realize you have taken a different stance. If consistency was not your pattern it will take time for them to believe in the changes. Again, remember a period of unpleasantness is an inevitable part of the process.

Another ... less abusive response can happen. Some of your family members will do their chores and others will be sympathetic to your overworked state; and some will begin praising you for all the past things you have done for them by leaving love notes, taking you out, baking you a cake or cooking your favorite food or bringing flowers. The charming stage will begin. Remember, it used to work when you talked about needing more help around the house.

Another ... thing that can happen will be that someone will begin doing your chores. This is to set up the, "I help you, why can't you help me?" syndrome. Be aware, because this action will only confuse and undermine your resolve to be in charge of the things you are willing to do. Again have a script ready when this happens. "I noticed you did one of my chores, I am puzzled, did you lose your list?" Let the person answer your question, don't answer for the person.

Another ... thing that can happen is the family meets to try and figure what's wrong with you; and together they may try to influence you by having a concerted effort to please you to get you back in place so they can go on with their lives as before.

Another ... thing that will happen is that you will need to ignore the chores that are not being done. You might have to buy paper plates and plasticware if someone is not doing dishes anymore. You might have to go to the store for your meals if the person who is in charge of grocery shopping is on strike. You might have to wash your own clothes if the laundry chore did not get resolved. You might have to buy a large plastic trash can or paper basket to put the clutter that is disturbing you because someone is not doing the daily pick up. You might have to eat your meals out if someone is not doing the cooking. Be prepared to follow through and know that they are waiting and predicting you will give in.

Another ... thing you can do is to set up a file for chores. Each week list the chores that need to be accomplished by a certain day. For instance on Monday the file sheet for the week is available and the chores need to be accomplished by Sunday evening at six p.m.

The easiest way to get volunteers is to present the chore sheet as a sign-up sheet. This allows the family members to choose chores they like and those that interest them. It also can foster a non-gender issue regarding chores. Date each list so that you will be able to refer to it as time goes along and get an idea of how often certain chores need to be accomplished. The sign-up sheet can be used to note the chores that are most disagreeable and later on at a family meeting, discussion on why they are disagreeable can be aired. It can also be a fact sheet when one of the children complains that the other always picks the same type of chores.

Instructions regarding the chores need to be provided and explained. A sheet at the beginning of the instructions should outline what type of products are to be used on different items.

Wood furniture gets cleaned with ____*(Furniture Oil).*____ Never use water. Use a soft, lint free cloth.

Glass is cleaned with __*(Vinegar)*__ using a lint free cloth, newspaper or paper towel.

Painted metal is cleaned with _____ Use absorbent cloth.

Toilets are cleaned with_____ Use brush and absorbent cloth.

Stainless steel sink is cleaned with _____ Never use cleanser. Use absorbent cloth.

Hardwood floors are cleaned with _____ Never use water.

Ceramic tile is cleaned with _____

Kitchen floor tile is cleaned with _____

The list can be signed by the first one up on Monday or in chronological order, youngest first, etc. or oldest first or draw the highest card or the lowest card. If there are three children in the house then you need to have an even number of chores. Fifteen chores to be accomplished will give them five each. Age will be a factor and if this is the case and you want the younger children to be participating, then a separate list for them needs to be developed. Decide at the onset what chores are reasonable for the age. The children younger than four, hopefully, will be imitating the *new order*. It will be useful to get them to put toys in the toy box, clothes in the drawer, fold washed clothes, "dust" and choose the clothes they want to wear.

Another thing the family can do at this point to disrupt the *new order* is to have accidents and do things the wrong way. Women normally overreact to this. It is probably the best way to get you to "do it right" and eventually get you to take over the chore again.

It can happen by breaking your favorite dish or object while cleaning or cooking or washing dishes. It can happen while doing the laundry and throwing your good white blouse in with the dark clothes or the towels. It can happen by over-watering your favorite plant. It can happen by losing something valuable. (See Chapter 11, Period of Unpleasantness) It can happen by not knowing where the pot is to cook or the bowl is to mix or the ingredients needed for a recipe.

Remember, you are through talking about getting help. If you are unable to resist "taking over so it gets done right," then begin to practice immediately. Know what you are going to do if the above crisis happens. Face it now!

The first clue that it is sabotage is to realize who cares that the chore was botched? Remember, you have the family meeting format to resolve problems and don't be tempted to "talk about it to other family members." Reaction is desired by the family members in order to get things back to normal; meaning you doing everything better." Have the courage to act instead of react," says Darlene Larson-Jenks. Always see this as a long term project and realize that the efforts in the past for quick fixes were not successful.

This list can also be used if you hire cleaning persons. It is initially a time consuming project to develop this organized list, but it will avoid costly mistakes and provide a place to add on new items as they occur.

Ideally, your husband will be supportive as a parent with the sign up approach to getting chores accomplished. If he is not supportive, go ahead anyway and act as if you expect this to work. Remember, you are through talking about getting help.

If your spouse is not supportive of the sign up sheet then you can expect some interference. This may appear by remarks such as, "Dad said I don't have to do it" or "Dad will give me phone messages, or let me use the car or have friends over." Ignore the remarks and don't take the bait or diversion. This is a family affair and the work needs to be divided. You are only talking about sign up sheets at family meetings.

Too often women hide behind, "yes, but" excuse of "my husband is not supportive." Remember, it is not likely that two people will wake up on the same day and decide that splitting chores evenly is a great idea. You are the one with the overload problem and therefore you are the one motivated to seek solutions and make the change. (See Chapter 9, Men and Women-Spouse Help)

Praise is the best way to ensure the progress of this new lifestyle. Use sentences that begin with, *When*, to praise family members. Make a concentrated effort to look for progress and verbalize the praise.

For example: When you do the dishes the kitchen looks nice. When you grocery shopped you did a great job. When you cut the grass the yard looks great. When you pick up your room it looks like a magazine picture.

Most of us are suspicious of praise because we realize that the person is judging us. If you word the praise so that it comments on the job well done they will not feel like they are being manipulated. The chore was expected to be done by you and you are telling them that they did well. Praise builds self-esteem. Criticism destroys self-esteem.

There needs to be a consequence for each person involved if they do not do the chores they agreed to do. You will have to decide that by what you know about the child. Restricting phone calls, car use, television time are useful. It is crucial they know the consequence in advance.

Getting through this period of unpleasantness is essential to getting help. When people are used to certain behaviors, they do not take you seriously when you say you are going to change. When we make New Year's resolutions for instance, no one expects you to keep them. It is even a subject for jokes. This is not a laughing matter for you. It is a matter of you being in charge of your life and staying well and happy. The loving thing to do is to get through these couple of weeks so that you get the help you need and spouse and mother can be seen as a calm and loving person.

The exercise on the next page will help you deal with this dilemma.

What is the worst thing I predict will happen by presenting the Sign-up sheets to my children? Review your family history in regard to change.

What am I afraid is going to happen?

_____

_____

_____

_____

What am I confident I can do by myself?

_____

_____

_____

_____

What am I resistant to?

_____

_____

_____

_____

What techniques am I going to use to make this work?

_____

_____

_____

_____

Who is going to be my woman support contact?

_____

_____

_____

What am I going to be doing to feel good about myself?

_____

_____

_____

_____

*****

Why did you read this chapter?

_____

_____

_____

What is your resistance to the suggestions for change?

_____

_____

_____

What techniques have you chosen to initiate change?

_____

_____

_____

When are you going to start? _____

Chapter 6

CHORES

"By and large, mothers and housewives are the only workers who do not have regular time off. They are the great vacation-less class."

-Anne Morrow-Lindbergh

Women are virtually unanimous that their roles should—and will—continue to change in the 1990s. As growing numbers of women discover that talking about shared housework responsibility is not getting the chores done, they will look for a plan of action and press for the change.

In order to implement a plan of action for shared housework and enable you to press for the change, the following lists have been designed so you can check off what you want to do. Duplicate the sheet for further discussion and decisions by the other family members, including your husband or significant other; and any other adults in the household.

KITCHEN

_____refrigerator inside
_____refrigerator outside
_____freezer
_____cabinets inside
_____cabinets outside
_____stove outside
_____oven inside
_____oven outside
_____microwave inside
_____microwave outside
_____shelves
_____under the counter appliances
_____counter appliances
_____hanging decorations
_____floor
_____walls
_____light fixtures
_____dishwasher outside
_____sink
_____table and chairs
_____counters
_____pantry
_____mirrors
_____windows
_____drapes/shades/blinds
_____doors

BREAKFAST ROOM

_____table and chairs
_____shelves
_____decorations
_____floor

_____walls
_____light fixtures
_____serving furniture
_____mirrors
_____doors
_____windows
_____drapes/shades/blinds

DINING ROOM

_____table and chairs
_____floor/carpet
_____walls
_____light fixtures
_____decorations
_____china cabinets
_____buffet
_____windows
_____drapes/shades/blinds
_____mirrors
_____doors

STUDY/DEN

_____desk
_____light fixtures
_____floor
_____walls
_____closets
_____bookcases
_____file cabinets
_____chairs
_____windows
_____drapes/shades/blinds

_____mirrors
_____doors

GREAT ROOM/LIVING ROOM

_____couch/sofa
_____chairs
_____tables
_____floor
_____light fixtures
_____decorations
_____fireplace inside
_____fireplace outside
_____fireplace equipment
_____wood gathering
_____windows
_____drapes/shades/blinds
_____walls
_____doors
_____entertainment center

FAMILY ROOM

_____couch/sofa
_____chairs
_____tables
_____floor
_____light fixtures
_____decorations
_____fireplace inside
_____fireplace outside
_____fireplace equipment
_____windows
_____drapes/shades/blinds

_____walls
_____doors
_____entertainment center
_____wood gathering

ENTRANCE HALL

_____door
_____windows
_____floor
_____walls
_____decorations
_____mirror
_____furniture
_____light fixtures

BEDROOM MASTER

_____door
_____windows
_____drapes/shades/blinds
_____floor
_____bed(s)
_____chair
_____furniture
_____mirror
_____entertainment center
_____decorations
_____closet
_____light fixtures

BEDROOM TWO

_____door

_____windows
_____drapes/shades/blinds
_____floor
_____bed(s)
_____chair
_____furniture
_____mirror
_____entertainment center
_____decorations
_____closet
_____light fixtures

BEDROOM THREE

_____door
_____windows
_____drapes/shades/blinds
_____floor
_____bed(s)
_____chair
_____furniture
_____mirror
_____entertainment center
_____decorations
_____closet
_____light fixtures

BEDROOM FOUR

_____door
_____windows
_____drapes/shades/blinds
_____floor
_____bed(s)

_____chair
_____furniture
_____mirror
_____entertainment center
_____decorations
_____closet
_____light fixtures

HOME OFFICE

_____door
_____windows
_____drapes/shades/blinds
_____floor
_____chairs
_____desk
_____light fixtures
_____computer equipment
_____decorations
_____closet
_____file cabinets
_____shelves

BATHROOM ONE

_____commode
_____sink
_____cabinet
_____mirror
_____decorations
_____shower door
_____tub
_____fixtures
_____floor

_____walls
_____door
_____light fixtures

BATHROOM TWO

_____commode
_____sink
_____cabinet
_____mirror
_____decorations
_____shower door
_____tub
_____fixtures
_____floor
_____walls
_____door
_____light fixtures

BASEMENT

_____misc
_____misc
_____misc

GARAGE

_____misc
_____misc
_____misc

ATTIC

_____misc
_____misc
_____misc

*****

Why did you read this chapter?

_____

_____

_____

What is your resistance to the suggestions for change?

_____

_____

_____

What techniques have you chosen to initiate change?

_____

_____

_____

When are you going to start? _____

Chapter 7

SAME 24 HOURS

"Too many activities, and people, and things. Too many worthy activities, valuable things, and interesting people. For it is not merely the trivial which clutters our lives but the important as well."

-Anne Morrow-Lindbergh

Women are perceived as being good managers of time because they accomplish so many things within each twenty-four hour period. This is wrong because being in charge of our twenty-four hours is not the same as accomplishing many things a day. Being in charge means we are doing what we want and need each day and measuring progress toward those goals. It is not being in charge of your life when you are doing for others what they should be doing for themselves; because you cannot say no, or feel guilty if you do say no, or have not valued yourself enough to establish your own goals.

There are many *time* messages in our language. Here are just a few, circle the ones that you use and write down others:

Time is money. Time out. Time flies. Time gets away from me. I run out of time. I spend too much time ... Someone is always wasting my time. I waste time doing ... Other people take my time. I don't have enough time. That was bad timing. My time is not my own. I am always late. Others are always late. There's always interruptions. It will only take a minute/second.

_____

_____

_____

_____

What is your reality of time? Do you have conflicts of time with other people, colleagues, friends, employees, family and parents? Remember you have the same twenty-four hours as the rest of the world and you are either managing it or time is managing you.

List twelve activities that take your time each day. Remember the values we discussed in Chapter 1, Double Jeopardy?

1. _____

2. _____

3. _____

4. _____

5. _____

6. _____

7. _____

8. _____

9. _____

10. _____

11. _____

12. _____

See Chapter 1 (Double Jeopardy) and Chapter 2 (What Do You Want?) where you decided what you *need and want*.. *Write a* **N or W** next to the activities that fit in your previous decision. Ask why you are doing the others.

Make a decision now of whether the activity belongs in your 24 hours. Yes or No. Now what will happen when you say no to this activity?

_____

_____

_____

_____

_____

How are you going to respond?

_____

_____

_____

_____

_____

_____

_____

Time management is a real key to change. What good is it; to do an inventory of what you want and need in life, identify the excuses that are your saboteurs; and then not follow through when your decisions affect other people? It is important to know what you want to say. Look at the past conversations and you will have an idea of what to expect. This is important so you will not use an excuse such as, "I was taken by surprise and I didn't know what to say." Write out your response and practice saying it out loud. This is very important because women have a tendency to speak in soft or whining voices and that gives the impression of a little girl unsure of her message. By practicing the response and keeping it in one to three sentences you will be heard and eventually taken seriously.

Remember you are trying to develop a new awareness of your reality as a woman and identify the excuses that disturb your balance so you can rekindle the spirit and joy in your life.

WHERE DOES THE TIME GO?

List the activity you plan to do and project the time you now think it will take. Time the activity and record the actual time. This exercise is extremely important because there is always a contradiction between how long we think an activity will take. At the end of each day, record **P - F** or **C** after each activity so you will be able to measure the amount of balance in your day. Recording actual time makes us aware of how we are actually spending our time and to be aware of why we are so tired. The following chart is a guide for your use.

A is *projected* time. **B** is *actual* time. Columns represent one hour. * C-*Career,* P-*Personal,* F-*Family*

*	Activity		Mon									
P	*TV*	A	1 hr									
		B	4 hr									
		A										
		B										
		A										
		B										
		A										
		B										
		A										
		B										
		A										
		B										
		A										
		B										
		A										
		B										
		A										
		B										
		A										
		B										
		A										
		B										

Keep this record for six weeks in order to get a clear picture of where your time goes. Remember, this is a long term project and cannot be fixed quickly. The more thorough you are developing this inventory, the better base decisions you can make to accomplish your wants and needs; and therefore get in charge of your time and energy.

Now let's take a few minutes and figure out how you are going to do this tracking. Can you carry this Activity Record Sheet everywhere you go? Where can you carry it? What are you going to use instead? It is suggested you carry 3x5 cards or a similar size notebook. Jot down when you begin an activity and when it ends. It would also be helpful to record the interruptions. Later, you will be able to get a clear picture of how these interruptions disrupt your management of time. Then you can decide what techniques to use to abort the interruptions.

There is a contradiction in what we think is happening and what is really happening. Gathering the facts about how we are spending our time helps us analyze how we really spend our time. Record your time every day. It will be helpful to put names with the interruptions so you can know who is "taking your time" or "wasting your time." These names will be needed in order to develop your responses in the future when you are developing your time management plan. In other words, now you are gathering the facts of the history of the days in your personal life, family life and career life. When you implement the change in your time management strategies, it will impact people on your list; and you'll want to be prepared with responses so you do not react to their whims. It is imperative the activity is recorded as soon as it is happens or your "time will get away."

Begin this project as soon as possible. It is a known fact that when we put off a project it is not likely to be started. Procrastination is an undesirable excuse.

Procrastination is seen in our society as an excuse not to get things done. It is accepted by almost everyone and even joked about as being a common problem. Procrastination is a serious problem because it really is the root of whether you are successful or not. It will be interesting to find out which areas of your life you procrastinate, and why. Each time you evaluate a time management project you will learn something about yourself. One dictionary's definition is "to put off habitually, until tomorrow, what should be done" also dawdle, delay and loiter.

Make a list of all the things you have wanted to do and needed to do in the last year.

_____

_____

_____

_____

_____

_____

_____

Now, write the reason why each was not accomplished. Be specific and thorough in this inventory because it will give you the insight you need to overcome the procrastination.

Write **P** - **F** - or **C** next to each item on the *previous page* in order to gather information about which areas you are procrastinating. List the people involved in the activity you did not accomplish.

_____

_____

_____

_____

_____

Do you procrastinate about everything?

_____

_____

_____

_____

_____

_____

_____

In which areas of your life do you procrastinate?

_____

_____

_____

_____

Which people are involved?

_____

_____

_____

_____

Procrastination is a behavior that you will need to change. What are the functions (payoffs) of procrastination for you in your past and now?

_____

_____

_____

_____

_____

Are you afraid of rejection? _____

Are you afraid of success? _____

Are you angry? _____

What are your effective, creative and feel good activities?

_____

_____

_____

_____

_____

List the activities you accomplish on a regular basis. Place a
P - F - C to alert you regarding areas of balance. It is also
important to measure progress and not solely concentrate on
the areas we have to improve in order to take charge of our
lives.

_____

_____

_____

_____

_____

One thing to be done regarding procrastination is to admit that it is a problem. Label the behavior, not yourself. It is unrealistic to expect everything to get done. No one gets everything done.

It is a psychological premise that what you resist - persists. Stop labeling yourself as a procrastinator. You are a woman and when you put off until tomorrow what should be done today, it is causing you a problem. It is culturally common for a woman to put off doing an activity that will be unpleasant or cause discomfort for others. When you are trying to manage your time you will need to be able to see the contradiction with pleasing other people and pleasing yourself. Change means that we have to do some things in our lives that will cause discomfort to others. This is not harmful and that needs to be clear in your mind. Discomfort of others is their feeling not yours. You cannot feel for two or more people, you can only feel for yourself in order to be truly happy and healthy.

Now that you have defined the areas and people involved in your procrastination problem, you need to have a plan to do something different and get past the fears, anger and external referencing (relationships, lack of boundaries, I'm a good girl and not trusting your own perceptions).

Make a game plan for changing each area you defined involving your procrastinating. Examples of game plans are: writing a script for a response if rejection was the reason; or writing a plan encompassing the time needed for an activity and a script response if you anticipate it causing someone discomfort; or expressing the anger toward a person in an appropriate way rather than not finishing a promised project; or being chronically late for appointments.

*****

Why did you read this chapter?

_____

_____

_____

What is your resistance to the suggestions for change?

_____

_____

_____

What techniques have you chosen to initiate change?

_____

_____

_____

When are you going to start? _____

Chapter 8

LET'S ENTERTAIN

"I know that for many people, giving a party is a penance. For me it is pure happiness, pure pleasure. I love giving parties. I always have. I always shall."

-Elsa Maxwell

*L*et's entertain. Sounds like a fun idea doesn't it? Then why is it so stressful? Let's look at your entertaining calendar for one year, including immediate family, family of origin, in-laws, friends, acquaintances, business, neighbors and drop-ins. For example:

Group	Occasion	Make Plans	Prep Time	Does Work
(Family)	*(Holiday Brunch)*	*(Me)*	*(8 hrs)*	*(Me)*

_____

_____

_____

_____

_____

_____

_____

_____

_____

_____

_____

Now that you have written the facts about your entertaining patterns, let's take the issue all the way through and find out what makes you angry and resentful and stressed out regarding entertaining. Remember, entertaining can be fun; and if it isn't, you are the only one that can change your environment and get in charge of having fun while entertaining.

Resentments and anger for women in the Virginia Slims Opinion Poll, means "having more control over the way things are going in my life" (cited by 28 percent of women and 30 percent of men). Also cited among married women, however, is more help with household responsibilities from their spouses: 26 percent say that this would improve their lives significantly. Another high priority item for all groups of women is more leisure time. It is cited by 25 percent of women. Other wishes? Seventeen percent of women would like to have less stress at home. Given those statistics, let's get more perspective on the stress of entertaining by doing the following exercise.

Review each group and determine what caused the glitch:

Group	What caused the glitch?	Changes to make!
(Family)	*(One family came late and we waited)*	*(Mail invitations with RSVP; & Eat on time)*

Describe your three *worst* entertainment scenarios.

(Arguments with spouse; last minute changes; uninvited guests)

_____

_____

_____

_____

_____

_____

_____

_____

_____

_____

_____

How long did the period of unpleasantness last? _____

What methods have you tried in the past to make entertaining less stressful for **YOU**?

_____

_____

_____

_____

_____

_____

What are the most unpleasant things that happen to you personally? (fights and arguments, no help, spouse taking credit for the preparation, embarrassing remarks by spouse during the entertainment, etc.)

_____

_____

_____

_____

_____

_____

_____

Here are some suggestions to make entertainment fun and less stressful. Know specifically why you are entertaining. Prepare on paper an accounting for all the needed food, decorations, seating, plates, time for food preparation, assistance for all preparation, special needs of guests, etc. Use 8 1/2" x 11" sheets for this work-up so you can file it in an entertainment file. You'll have it for reference the next occasion for the same group. Use this sheet to remark on the success of the party, favorite food and drink of the guests, as well as notes of what went wrong and what to try to do different the next time.

Before you begin to activate the plan, have a family meeting. If it is a family occasion let the family members know of the scheduled occasion and ask for input and clearly ask each member "what are you going to be responsible for in preparing for this occasion?" Be sure to include yourself in the input discussion, especially by clearly letting them know what you are willing to do. In the event they do not come through with their responsibilities let that item out. This will seem uncomfortable at first but it really is not such a crisis. Women want the area of their home and family to be less stressful according to the Virginia Slims Opinion Poll. This is an excellent way to relieve some of the stress. Remember, that your family is not used to you being consistent regarding responsibility in the home and accountability afterwards. If you "take it back," you will be getting what you "asked for" but not what you need.

If there is no family, and you and your husband are doing the entertaining as a couple, then many of the previous suggestions still apply. It is interesting though to evaluate the excuses we make for the spouse not following through. Basically, you need to still ask for your spouse's input in the entertainment projection, clearly ask what he will be responsible for and clearly say what you are going to be responsible for. Now if there are any blanks, further options need to be considered;

such as hiring help, doing without, changing the plan or asking for assistance from the guest(s). Again, let's emphasize the importance of careful planning, spouse/family input, clear requests for shared responsibility, clear message of your responsibilities and how you plan to account for any missing responsibilities.

*****

Why did you read this chapter?

_____

_____

_____

What is your resistance to the suggestions for change?

_____

_____

_____

What techniques have you chosen to initiate change?

_____

_____

_____

When are you going to start? _____

Chapter 9

Men and Women - Spouse Help

"Anger repressed can poison a relationship as surely as the cruelest words."

-Joyce Brothers

*O*ngoing polls by Virginia Slims indicate that women are angrier than ever at their men. This has been rising steadily since 1970. When women were asked: what would make their life better? More money, 60 percent; More control over way things are going in my life, 28 percent; More help with household chores from spouse, 26 percent.

When asked: what causes the most resentment ... Amount of money there is to live on, 63 percent; How much my mate helps me around the house, 52 percent; the way my job or career has gone, 49 percent; not having enough free time, 49 percent and how I look, 48 percent.

This anger and resentment is affecting the men and children in their lives. One of the "improvements" in the 1990 poll is that men are talking different regarding what would make life better, but the fact of the matter is, they are not doing their share of household chores.

Do women really feel more resentment than men? The answer is a resounding, yes, at least in several key aspects of life. The widest gaps are in the areas of:

... How much their mate helps out around the house (52 percent of women say they feel resentful at least from time to time, versus only 27 percent of men);

... How they look (48 percent versus 29 percent);

... The way child-care related duties are shared in their households (46 percent versus 22 percent).

Women are more critical of men today than they were 20 years ago. Asked in the Virginia Slims Opinion Poll, to say whether various descriptions of men were mostly accurate or not, more women today than in 1970 choose to portray men in a negative light on almost every item.

In particular, women are far more likely now to say that most men look at a woman and immediately think about what it would be like to go to bed with her; or that most men are interested in their work and life outside the home and don't pay much attention to things going on at home. Women are far less likely than they were 20 years ago to say that most men are basically kind, gentle, and thoughtful.

Women's opinions about men: (1st % represents 1990, 2nd % represents 1970)

Most men think only their own opinions about the world are important. (58%/50%)

Most men find it necessary for their egos to keep women down. (55%/49%)

Most men look at a woman and immediately think how it would be to go to bed with her. (54%/41%)

Most men are interested in their work and life outside the home and don't pay much attention to things going on at home. (53%/39%)

Most men are basically kind, gentle, and thoughtful. (51%/67%)

Most men are more interested in their own, rather than a woman's, sexual satisfaction. (50%/40%)

Most men are basically selfish and self-centered. (42%/32%)

Why are women increasingly critical of men? It is unlikely that men are objectively more selfish and self-centered than they were in 1970; men's actual conduct, if anything, probably has improved.

What has changed is women's sense of their proper entitlement. As more men and women have abandoned traditional roles, an attempt to negotiate new terms for their relationships, women's expectations have shifted. The more independent women of today expect more from men and want more out of relationships.

Not surprisingly, behavior regarded as sexist in 1970 bothers even greater numbers of American women today. More than half of women say they are bothered by every example of sexism asked about in the Virginia Slims Opinion Poll.

For example, Eight in 10 women today say it annoys them when "a woman is looked at as a sex symbol instead of as having sense in her head."

Does this make you angry? _____

How do you handle this situation?

_____

_____

What will you do in the future?

_____

_____

_____

_____

Three-quarters get annoyed at women being left home while men go out for a good time.

Does this make you angry? _____

How do you handle this situation?

_____

_____

What will you do in the future?

_____

_____

_____

_____

Sixty-one percent are irritated by pictures of nude women in men's magazines.

Does this make you angry? _____

How do you handle this situation?

_____

_____

What will you do in the future?

_____

_____

_____

_____

More than half (53 percent) are bothered when a man talks about them as a girl and not a woman.

Does this make you angry? _____

How do you handle this situation?

_____

_____

What will you do in the future?

_____

_____

_____

An equal number (53 percent) don't like jokes about women drivers, mothers-in-law, or dumb blondes.

Does this make you angry? _____

How do you handle this situation?

_____

_____

_____

What will you do in the future?

_____

_____

_____

What would women most like to change in men? More able to express feelings. (27 percent)

What would men most like to change in women? More able to express feelings. (23 percent)

Family responsibilities are more likely to affect a woman's job than a man's. Husbands and wives do not share such burdens equally. For instance, when asked what happens when their child's day-care arrangements fall through, working mothers are twice as likely as their male counterparts (fathers with working wives) to say that it causes problems for them at work. In other words, the worker, mother, wife is more likely to pick up the slack than the worker, father, husband.

Does this make you angry? _____

How do you handle this situation?

_____

_____

What alternatives do you see for the future?

_____

_____

_____

Would you consider a standby person to be on call when this situation occurs?

_____

Who can you call on when a child is ill and needs to stay home?

_____

Who can you call on when a child has a doctor appointment?

_____

When you have a Plan-B (alternative plan) for likely situations, you are only a phone call away from avoiding a work crisis.

What is preventing you from having a Plan-B for your children?

_____

Of course, having more money for women would relieve some stress at the household and child care levels. With more money comes more power and consequently you could choose to hire help.

Married women (26 percent) say that more help with household responsibilities from their husbands, would improve their lives significantly.

According to the Virginia Slims Opinion Poll of 1990, women are more critical of men today that they were in the 70s.

So, women are getting angrier and angrier. After awhile unresolved anger turns to resentment. It is difficult if not impossible to be consumed with anger and resentment and try to love at the same time. It is a contradiction.

What are your choices?

1. Wait until the man in your life becomes more sensitive to your needs.

2. Threaten divorce.

3. Fight and argue about what you want to change.

4. Talk negatively to your children about their father not sharing of the household chores.

5. Hiring someone to do the other household chores.

6. Hiring someone to do your household chores.

7. Complain to your family, friends, neighbors and workplace people about your husbands lack of shared household chores.

8. Say you not going to do certain chores and within a predictable length of time, you take the chores on.

9. Say you are going to be responsible for specific chores and then follow through with only those specific chores.

10. Say you are going to be responsible for specific chores and then take on the ones your spouse "doesn't do right."

Remember, that for a long time you have been talking about needing shared responsibility for household chores. You are the one who needs to have this changed. Male spouses are used to asking for help. The polls show they are becoming more sensitive to that being a legitimate request. There is no need for them to change, since you keep doing the chores. One thing different is that the years of anger are taking a toll on many male/female relationships. What are your goals for your relationship? Is there a contradiction in what you want in the relationship and the inconsistencies you project in your requests for shared household responsibilities?

Review your family of origin and be aware of how chores were distributed. Were complaints made about chores and your father, but never resolved? Were fights and arguments made between parents over chores? Were punishments in the form of breaking things, stealing, hiding or physical violence, a product of your mother wanting to change the chore imbalance? Know why you do not follow through so you can determine what to change?

A passive sweet man often chooses a hostile woman. Then he uses her anger to avoid having to confront his own anger. When she gets angry, he doesn't have to. Eventually, this causes problems because if he doesn't like hostility in himself, he won't like it in his spouse either.

Review Chapter 6 on Chores, and decide what you are going to do in the areas of household chores.

Inform your spouse of your "lifestyle" and get a life.

If your spouse notices that certain household chores are not being done, and asks you, "when are you going to get it cleaned up?", be prepared to answer, "It was not on my to-do list." If he asks more questions, reply by asking him, what is it you don't understand about my answer? Remember, that you did inform him of your share in the household chores. There should be no reason to explain any further in an adult to adult relationship. If you have assumed a parent-child relationship, when you answer as if your spouse was your parent, then there are other issues that need to be resolved.

Be prepared for a period of unpleasantness to follow because you are doing something different. Review past conversations with your spouse and predict the type of behavior he uses to get you to change your mind. If breaking things or stealing or hiding things is his "punishment" for getting in charge of your life, then be prepared to have mechanisms in place for accountability. (See Chapter 11, Period of Unpleasantness) If you predict physical violence as his method of getting you to change your mind, then you will need to protect yourself.

*****

Why did you read this chapter?

_____

_____

_____

What is your resistance to the suggestions for change?

_____

_____

_____

What techniques have you chosen to initiate change?

_____

_____

_____

When are you going to start? _____

Chapter 10

DON'T ASK QUESTIONS

"When she stopped conforming to the conventional picture of femininity she finally began to enjoy being a woman"
-Betty Naomi Friedan

*M*any disagreements begin because we ask questions. Sounds weird but it's true. Think about the questions we ask of men. How many of them are childlike and nonsensical and rote? Over the years as you were growing up you were told by your mother to "go ask your father." Important questions were asked of the father. In a room full of people, women will invariably address important questions to males. It happens in the home, socially and in the office. Men also ask other men important questions. When you become aware of this society glitch you can change it.

Women notice this phenomenon after getting married. Here we have a woman that has lived alone and been raising her family for a period of time, making home decisions on a regular basis and she becomes a "questioner" as a wife.

For instance: Who do you think I should call to repair the sink? What do you think we should do about the noisy neighbor? Where should I take my car to get tuned up? Does the washer sound like it is making a funny noise? Did you hear someone at the door? What would you like for dinner? Do you like this dress? Does the house look nice?

What to do? Answer the question yourself. It is okay to change your mind. While you are trying to change this questionable habit, say something like: "Never mind I know that answer or Never mind I know what to do." If you are a parent, you are demonstrating this *incompetence* role to your sons and daughters.

What questions do you habitually ask of your spouse?

(Can you fix this? ... how do you like this outfit?)

_____

_____

_____

What questions do you habitually ask of your father?

_____

_____

_____

What questions do you habitually ask of the men in your workplace?

_____

_____

_____

What questions do you habitually ask of your mother?

_____

_____

_____

What questions do you habitually ask of the women in your workplace?

_____

_____

_____

Evaluate your reasons for choosing these people to answer your questions?

_____

_____

_____

_____

_____

_____

_____

_____

_____

What can you do differently?

_____

_____

_____

_____

_____

If women are to be taken seriously and listened to, they must act like women, speak like women, use body language like women; and above all give a clear message that they mean what they say.

*****

Why did you read this chapter?

_____

_____

_____

What is your resistance to the suggestions for change?

_____

_____

_____

What techniques have you chosen to initiate change?

_____

_____

_____

When are you going to start? _____

Chapter 11

PERIOD OF UNPLEASANTNESS

"In anxiety-provoking situations, many women feel unable to act. They find themselves at a loss to come up with an effective response, or any response at all."
                                        -Stanlee Phelps and Nancy Austin

W ith change comes a period of unpleasantness. Some experts say without pain there is no gain. It is useful to know what personal sabotage in your life causes you not to change. Procrastination is an issue, but not the core reason for not following through.

When you are the only one that decides to do something different, it is going to effect the other people in your life. It is not realistic that others will agree at the same moment to change an area of their lives. In Harriet Goldhor Lerner's book, The Dance of Anger, she says, "We cannot make another person change his or her steps to an old dance, but if we change our own steps, the dance no longer can continue in the same predictable pattern." It is also important to get in charge of your steps to becoming comfortable with change.

Since many of us are making these boundaries (steps) for the first time, it can feel scary for everyone involved.

Are any of the following statements familiar?

"Quit nagging"

"You always complain about something"

Ignore you

Point out things you are doing wrong

Make fun and mimic your new responses

Withhold sex

Refuse to do something financial

"You're just making a mountain out of a molehill"

"You sound like your mother, she's never satisfied"

"Quit pushing your luck"

"You're lucky I don't leave, then you'd really know how good you've got it"

What are the ways the people in your life discourage you from changing?

_____

_____

_____

_____

_____

_____

_____

_____

When you are verbally threatened, you experience fear. Fear can paralyze you. When you are paralyzed there is no action. Be aware of the strategy involved during this period of unpleasantness. Watch for the body language and tone/melody of the voice. In stressful situations, we pay attention to body language and voice, 90 percent; and in regular situations, 65 percent.

This knowledge will help you stay on track and actively keep you pursuing the change strategy you have outlined for yourself. Be optimistic that the change you are making will make you more in charge of your life and your destiny. You have the right to change.

Look at your personal history. List the things you have tried to change in the past five years.

This year _____

Last year _____

Two years ago _____

Three years ago _____

Four years ago _____

Five years ago _____

Review the list and write in the margin why the change did not come about.

Begin by answering the following questions on paper or in this book.

Who was involved? _____

_____

What happened during the period of unpleasantness?

_____

_____

How many days did you stick with the proposed change?

_____

Did you have a plan of action? _____

Why did you tell yourself you didn't change?

_____

What did you tell others?

_____

_____

Where was the change taking place?

Home/Work/Marriage/Parenting/Family of Origin/Friend

_____

_____

Now evaluate your history and determine if you still want to change any of the above resolutions. If you do, prioritize them below:

1. _____

2. _____

3. _____

4. _____

5. _____

6. _____

7. _____

Take into consideration the personal sabotage you have just reviewed and develop a plan for implementing the change.

_____

_____

_____

_____

Who are you going to tell about your plan to change? Please make sure it is someone you trust and that is on your team.

The reason for telling another person is so we can be accountable for activating the plan and be supported in our progress and cheered when successfully completed.

What to do when a family member steals and/or breaks your things.

Ask yourself:

Do you have a family member that steals from you?

Do you have personal objects broken or missing?

Do you wonder if you have misplaced the objects?

Do you think you are doing something wrong or it wouldn't be happening to you?

Do you feel disbelief that individual would really break or steal from you?

Do you have trouble confronting the suspected person because you are afraid more objects will be stolen or broken?

Did your mother/father throw away or break your possessions?

Do you keep this a secret?

Do you feel guilty about accusing your spouse, child, parent, sibling?

Have you tried to confront the suspected person but ended up being questioned and accused yourself? For instance, the suspected person might say to you: When was the last time you saw it? You probably just misplaced it, like you do your glasses all the time. Who else has been here? Who would want any of your junk? or a parent who said: "That will teach you to behave" or "Now you know how it feels" or "so and so needs this more than you do." Do you decide, that if it happens one more time, you will do something about it but find an excuse not too?

Have you tried family meetings to bring it into the open but the stealing and breaking continue to occur?

Do other family members have objects broken or stolen?

If a family member is stealing and breaking your things, allow yourself to feel hurt, pain, sadness, anger, shame, embarrassment because someone you love and supposedly loves you, is stealing and breaking your personal objects.

Trust yourself to know, it is a personal violation and that by confronting the behavior, you are doing what is right for you; and therefore the loving thing for the suspected family member. This is regardless of whether the suspected person is your spouse, child, parent or sibling.

The truth of the matter is, that by allowing the behavior to continue, you have been giving indirect permission for the family member to abuse you in this way. Once you get past the denial to what is happening to your property and you're not imagining it or think you're going crazy; then it will be possible to diffuse the actions of the family member. This is very important in building your confidence to confront these kind of violations. In order to break the denial about this behavior, take a pen or pencil and answer the *previous questions.* After answering the questions, you will be able to stay in your Real World and determine the options needed to stop the violation of your property.

Here are some options to consider:

Present the issue at a family meeting and let the family know the particulars. Come to the meeting with the list of stolen and/or broken items. Describe the item and let them know of its money value and also its personal value to you. Have this prepared in three sentences. It is beneficial that you rehearse what you are going to say so that you sound convincing and sure of the violation.

Let each member take a turn to express what they think can be done to stop the violation. Some of the family members will feel uncomfortable and will be reluctant to participate in the discussion. It is possible that they will strongly object and be angry that you are bringing it to their attention.

The family members will also react strongly to any suggestion that they "snitch" on their parent, spouse, sibling or child. This is predictably true if the family pattern has been to ignore unpleasant issues. Let the family know that you will no longer tolerate the violation and that there will be consequences if it happens again. Please do not bluff and be ready to list the consequences you have decided on. It is also important that you stay in charge of this portion of the meeting and not be diverted by blaming, distracting or placating language behavior.

Possible consequences to suggest:

1) Money to be taken out of a general fund or savings to replace or repair the object stolen or broken so the consequence will be felt by the family.

2) Make a report to the police, stating the personal damage and/or stolen article. This will be considered an unusual procedure by the law enforcement agency, but you are primarily interested in stopping the violation and not having it become a family secret. Be firm in your decision to insist that it be written and signed.

3) When you are convinced you know who is the culprit, you have the option to break or steal an object belonging to that person. Some experts believe to "put the shoe on the other foot" deters further violations.

4) Knowing the violator, you also have the option of replacing or repairing the object out of that person's account. This makes the consequence their Real World.

Tell the person that you forgive them for the violation and tell them how you felt to have something of yours broken or stolen. Tell the person that you believe there is something seriously wrong for them to resort to that kind of violation and suggest that they seek professional help to learn how to express themselves in socially acceptable ways. It is not the loving thing to do, if you allow a passive/aggressive behavior or other behavior type to have an excuse to steal or break your personal objects. It is wrong and it is a personal violation.

5) When you are not able to confront the issue, I would suggest that you work with your mentor, trusted mature friend and/or hire a specialist to work with you until you are able to confront the violator.

6) It is possible to look back at the events prior to the stealing or breaking of the objects, to determine some clues to who is the violator. By recording events, you can see "who had the motive" and use that information in confrontations. For instance, when your husband gets really angry at you, because you didn't do something he asked, you will be the victim of a broken or stolen object. In a confrontation, his question of "why do you think it's me," can be answered by saying, "you were the one that was angry."

7) When the objects mysteriously turn up after the confrontation, it is still necessary to confront in a family meeting. Don't let anyone divert you to believe that you misplaced, lost, or that you're crazy. Blaming is the most frequently used behavior in our society.

8) When your resistance to moving in the Real World is strong, you can choose to do the violator's inventory; and talk about passive/aggressive behaviors or other character defects that will allow you to feel superior, but will not help you move through the Real World. It is not useful to do the other person's inventory because that person has already justified the behavior and is receiving a payoff. You are the one that has been violated and you are the one that needs to find the resolution.

9) When your resistance to moving in the Real World is strong, you can choose to make excuses for the violator, such as: "having a bad day" or "is a child of an alcoholic" or "I'll

get over it" or "it probably is a phase" or "since it is my mother/father, it's history now" or "maybe I deserved it."

Be ready to experience a period of unpleasantness in the family. Family members will be uncomfortable with the "cat being out of the bag" and will be hoping to have the issue just "go away" and will want to pretend like it never happened. Someone might take the side of the accused and try to rationalize he/she was justified in their actions. Someone might be afraid to be supportive of what you are doing because it is also happening to them. Someone might be afraid because they need something from the accused: money, sex, transportation, help with children, physical abuse, fear of not being loved. Someone might just make excuses for the suspected person.

Johanna Spyri gives a good description regarding angry behavior in Heidi, Chapter 23, "Anger has overpowered him and driven him to a revenge which was rather a stupid one, I must acknowledge, but anger makes us all stupid."

What to do when a family member steals and breaks your things?

Trust yourself. Choose an option that will help you move into the Real World and be willing to go through the period of unpleasantness, one day at a time. It is the loving thing to do.

Write out your game plan for dealing with the methods each family member uses with you.

Name _____

_____

_____

_____

_____

Name_____

_____

_____

_____

_____

Name_____

_____

_____

_____

_____

Name_____

_____

_____

_____

DOMESTIC VIOLENCE is also a reason used to avoid taking charge of your life. It is not considered to be a period of unpleasantness because of the physical violence and danger. It is related to the verbal abuse and therefore needs to be acted on.

*****

Why did you read this chapter?

_____

_____

_____

What is your resistance to the suggestions for change?

_____

_____

_____

What techniques have you chosen to initiate change?

_____

_____

_____

When are you going to start? _____

Chapter 12

EXCUSE JOURNAL

"When people make changes in their lives in a certain area, they may start by changing the way they talk about that subject, how they act about it, their attitude toward it, or an underlying decision concerning it."

-Jane Illsley Clark

W hy aren't you changing the things in your life that will make your life easier?

(Won't work)

_____

_____

_____

_____

_____

Why are you holding on to the resentments against your husband, children, friends, family, co-workers and employers?
(Keep the peace)

_____

_____

_____

_____

_____

When you analyze your list you will see that there are two reasons for not changing. One is fear and the other is sickness. The fact that you have not dealt with the original anger and now have a resentment, is proof of fear or sickness. Why else would you not channel the anger to action?

_____

_____

_____

_____

_____

It is helpful to look at the women in your life to check if you are adopting their excuses for not being personally responsible for your life and therefore angry and resentful with others.

What was your maternal grandmother like? Was she happy or tense? How often was she sick with headaches/depression? Did she have hobbies, friends, work outside the home? What excuses did your grandmother use?

_____

_____

_____

_____

_____

_____

What was your mother like: Was she happy or tense? How often was she sick with headaches/depression? Did she have hobbies, friends, work outside the home? What excuses did your mother use?

_____

_____

_____

_____

_____

_____

Please list the excuses *you* are using today.

_____

_____

_____

_____

_____

_____

_____

As you read the chapters in this book, return to this journal and continue to identify your excuses. The excuses are your personal sabotage. They are clouding the solution and allowing you to continue to live in the stressful situation.

Scenario: A 70 year old woman complaining that she can't do what she wants because she can't drive. Her excuse for not driving is that her husband wouldn't teach her. This excuse has been used for over 50 years. This is a resentment in the highest degree. There is nothing physically wrong with this woman, so sickness is ruled out as the reason for not driving. Now that she is older she wants family and friends to take her places. She uses Verbal Abuse such as "Everyone understands why you don't have time to take me places" or "Even X's daughter has time to spend with her mother."

The options for her transportation at 70 years old are basically the same as 50 years ago; take professional driving lessons; take one of the offers from family members to teach her to drive; pay someone to take her places (chauffeur on call); taxi; trade-offs for someone else's driving offers with cake baking, etc. The message here is, when we are angry because we didn't get what we expected from a husband, we have choices. If you do not examine your excuses you will have a resentment. When your pattern is to make excuses, you will become mean and hateful to your husband and therefore cause more stress. Loving behavior and anger/resentment do not co-exist. Oprah Winfrey said, "I've discovered a lot of revelations about myself. I keep a journal and I've watched myself grow. I remember writing in my journal at twenty-five: 'I'm just so restless ... I should be doing more with my life and I'm not'."

JOURNAL FOR EXCUSES

EXCUSE	DATE	PERSON	FEAR	CHOICE

*****

Why did you read this chapter?

_____

_____

_____

What is your resistance to the suggestions for change?

_____

_____

_____

What techniques have you chosen to initiate change?

_____

_____

_____

When are you going to start? _____

Chapter 13

JUST DO IT

"The bottom line is that I am responsible for my own well-being, my own happiness. The choices and decisions I make regarding my life directly influence the quality of my days.
                                                          -Kathleen Andrus

Sometimes it's better not to think so much about the things that you are unhappy about. Thinking does not bring about change, but can get you angry. It can renew resentments and can be depressing. It is not surprising that more women are depressed that men. It is crucial that you get past the thinking stage of your unhappiness. Sounds too difficult? When you do not have a plan to implement your goals, it is difficult. The simple solution to your unhappy state is to develop a plan; and then follow it. What changes can make it easier for you to be in charge of your life? What complaints have you made in the past? When did change take place? When did things stay the same?

Let's break up into *three* categories: Household Chores; Other Activities and Parental Responsibilities.

List the *Household Chores* you do in the home. Take a clip board and use a separate sheet for each room, basement, attic, front and back yard, garage, etc.

_____

_____

_____

_____

_____

_____

_____

List the *Other Activities* you do, home entertainment - auto care - vacation - shopping - finances - family outings - animal care - holidays - repair appointments - Dr/Dentist appointments - caregiver - errands - etc. (use separate sheets)

_____

_____

_____

_____

_____

_____

_____

List your *Parental Responsibilities* in the home and outside the home. Remember to include school activities, sports and dancing, transportation, homework, PTA, conferences etc.

_____

_____

_____

_____

_____

_____

_____

Analyze the above, keeping in mind where you are trying to live up to other people's expectations and values, and take charge of your twenty-four hours by choosing the Household Chores,Other Activities and Parental Responsibilities. When these base decisions are made you will be able to have Personal Time in your life and be able to balance Career, Family and Personal time.

Write out the *three* sentences you will use to give a clear message of what you will be doing in the future.

(Please listen to what I'm saying. In the future I'll be responsible for the following. Here is a copy for your reference.)

_____

_____

_____

_____

_____

_____

_____

_____

Practice saying the message out loud and in front of the mirror. It is crucial that your verbal message corresponds with the body language and tone of voice.

Remember, you are looking for a change that you are in charge of. You will be able to open the door of the "gerbil cage." You will be in charge of your life.

Household chores you will now choose to do:

_____

_____

_____

_____

_____

_____

_____

_____

_____

_____

_____

_____

_____

Three sentence script to give your clear message:

_____

_____

_____

_____

_____

_____

_____

Other Activities you will <u>now</u> choose to do:

_____

_____

_____

_____

_____

_____

_____

Three sentence script to give your clear message:

_____

_____

_____

_____

_____

_____

_____

Parental Responsibilities you will <u>now</u> choose to do:

_____

_____

_____

_____

_____

_____

_____

Three sentence script to give your clear message:

_____

_____

_____

_____

_____

_____

Pearl Bailey, best known for her easy-going style, said in her book <u>Hurry Up America and Spit</u>, "We must change in order to survive."

*****

Why did you read this chapter?

_____

_____

_____

What is your resistance to the suggestions for change?

_____

_____

_____

What techniques have you chosen to initiate change?

_____

_____

_____

When are you going to start? _____

Chapter 14

WORK EXPECTATIONS

"Make (your employers) understand that you are in their service as workers, not as women."
-Susan Brownell Anthony

*I*t is in the workplace that women report both the greatest improvements over the past two decades and the greatest need for improvement in the years ahead. Women are twice as likely to acknowledge improvement in the workplace than in their roles as mothers, spouses, and homemakers. For the first time, a majority of women who work full-time report that they regard work as a career rather than just a job.

Women also experience growing levels of dissatisfaction, resentment, and stress related to their work, their earnings, their bosses, and their prospects for advancement.

At work, as in the home, women's expectations have risen over the past 20 years. A generation after they began crowding into the labor force, women are finding upward progress slower and harder than earlier anticipated. In 1970, 50 percent of women agreed that women are discriminated against in obtaining executive jobs in business. In 1990, 61 percent agreed.

In the work world, men are not significantly more satisfied than women with their employer or boss, or income. However, more men than women (by a 36 to 30 percent margin) say they are very satisfied with their future job prospects.

Women's and men's attitudes toward discrimination have differed somewhat over the 20 year history of the Virginia Slims Opinion Poll. More women than men perceive discrimination against women. But like women, more men today than in 1970 say that women are discriminated against in a variety of job-related situations.

According to the Virginia Slims Opinion Poll; Women say the following things have improved in the workplace ... The kinds of jobs open to women ... The salaries women are paid compared with what men are paid ... Women's opportunities for leadership positions in business ... The day-care options available to working mothers ... Women's opportunities for leadership positions in government.

Yet, they say further changes are needed to make their lives better ... The salaries women are paid compared with what men are paid ... The day-care options available to working mothers ... Women's opportunities for leadership positions in government ... Women's opportunities for leadership positions in business ... The kinds of jobs open to women ...

Aside from money, the Virginia Slims Opinion Poll discovered that women found the following things would make their jobs more/somewhat more satisfying: Incentive or bonus programs for higher productivity ... Better health benefits (HMOs, more medical coverage, dental coverage) ... Being under less pressure at work ... More flexible work hours (flextime, voluntary part-time, job sharing, leaves) ... More feedback from boss/manager.

Since a majority of employed women (53 percent) think of their work as just as jobs and a majority of men, 57 percent think of their work as careers, it is not surprising that women are finding dissatisfaction in the workplace. When people consider work as careers, they will expect their careers to progress. When people have jobs, they will not feel in charge of their workplace destiny.

Let's review your views about the workplace and determine whether it is a job or a career.

Why are you working?

_____

_____

When will you retire?

_____

What do you like about your career/job?

_____

_____

_____

_____

What is your projected time frame for your job/career advancement? Develop this in phases as appropriate.

_____

_____

_____

_____

_____

Do you have a job or a career?

_____

Are you on target today with these goals?

_____

Are you using a mentor to achieve your goals?

_____

Name the women in your workplace that are achieving their workplace goals:

_____

_____

_____

_____

Name the other acquaintances in similar workplace positions, that are achieving their goals:

_____

_____

_____

_____

_____

_____

_____

Name other women you know, friends, relatives, neighbors that are achieving their workplace goals:

_____

_____

_____

_____

_____

_____

_____

Name the women you associate with that are whiners rather
than winners in the workplace:

_____

_____

_____

_____

_____

_____

_____

Why do you stay in a relationship with a whiner?

_____

_____

_____

_____

_____

_____

_____

_____

What prevents you from reaching your goals? (fatigue, anger, money, unhappy relationships home or work, ill health, transportation, location, boss/supervisor, day care, other ...)

_____

_____

_____

State the specific reasons you are on target:

_____

_____

_____

_____

_____

State the specific reasons you are not on target:

_____

_____

_____

_____

_____

A mentor can make a remarkable breakthrough for a stalled career. A mentor gives upward mobility to career by speaking well of you to her peers. A mentor boosts self-esteem by believing in you. This gives you renewed confidence. A mentor shares your dreams. She can help you map out a plan of action and assist you in making your plan come true. A mentor gives vision. The mentor shares her vision and insights in life thereby stimulating you to stretch for higher goals. A mentor provides advice, counsel, and support. Supports you in crisis, and gives advise on new positions. A mentor introduces you to the corporate structure, its politics and players. A mentor teaches by example. A mentor imparts valuable information, not readily available. A mentor gives feedback on your progress.

When don't you need a mentor? When you are content or when the organizational structure is "in place" and no one is jockeying for positions. This happens most often in family businesses or when leaders are young. If you feel you are bumping the glass ceiling and all avenues have been exhausted including having a mentor, then you need to evaluate your career plan and decide what other options are there for you. Volunteering to be a member of a Board of Directors is a way of investigating other avenues. Most well run boards have a diverse profile, giving you information and provides a network for possible career choices.

*****

Why did you read this chapter?

_____

_____

_____

What is your resistance to the suggestions for change?

_____

_____

_____

What techniques have you chosen to initiate change?

_____

_____

_____

When are you going to start? _____

Chapter 15

MAINLY MONEY

"To be ignorant of money workings is to remain an outsider, a powerless outsider, to an enormously significant aspect of daily life."

-Judith Briles 1988

When women were asked in the Virginia Slims Opinion Poll, "What would make life better?", 60 percent said that having more money would make their lives better. When asked if given the chance to improve their relationship, what one aspect would people most like to change? Finances and the amount of time they spend with their mate were cited.

Sixty-three percent of women and 61 percent of men, now consider financial security to be part of a good marriage today, compared with only 49 percent of both groups in 1974. Having similar ideas on How to Handle Money is cited by 71 percent of women and 65 percent of men today, compared to 68 percent of women and 61 percent of men in 1974.

Women and Financial Management. If you never have enough money to make ends meet, chances are you're not becoming wealthier and you're not on a personal budget. Why not? Is it because:

.... "Budgets don't work"

.... "I'm not good at numbers"

.... "I don't have time"

.... "Credit cards"

.... "Everyone's in debt"

.... "My kids can't be deprived"

.... "My partner won't talk about money"

.... "There are always emergencies and surprises"

Having control over our finances is a conscious or unconscious choice we make. If you want to change your financial situation, begin by examining your attitudes about money. They have been influenced and shaped by your family, people you have relationships with, society, and your own sense of self-worth, to name just a few. Look at your relationships. How do the people in your life affect the choices you make regarding grocery shopping, the career you pursue, purchases of furniture, and insurance policies? Do you spend your money taking care of other people. but won't buy yourself a blouse because you "don't deserve" one? Do you hand over your buying power to your partner and play the victim?

Traditionally, women have been raised to believe that:

a) The needs of others comes first.

b) It is not feminine to be powerful or in control.

Becoming financially successful or wealthy requires taking care of yourself first, and establishing control over your own finances. It also requires shedding old ideas and developing a new outlook. What it necessitates is planning a personal budget. It may seem like a monumental task, but it's not if you take it one step at a time.

One way to ensure that your plan will work is to write down specific goals. Use the following outline.

1) List your immediate goals. *(one goal could be to plan that personal budget)*

2) How much money do you want to have invested or saved in: one to two years? two to five years? ten years? twenty years? thirty years? for retirement? To reach these goals, you must gain control over how you spend your money now.

Taking an inventory of personal expenses is the easiest and most accurate way of identifying how and why you spend your money. Most people resist this exercise, because it involves facing the truth about spending habits and attitudes about money, that may be holding you back.

To do your inventory, jot down what you spent money on at the end of each day, for six weeks. Be honest! List transportation, breakfast, lunch, dinner, coffee breaks, magazines and newspapers, personal care products, entertainment, etc. This will tell you what you personally need to live on comfortable. It will also eliminate the need to borrow from others, write unplanned checks, dip into sayings, or use credit cards in order to meet your everyday needs. You will see exactly what you spend your money on; and how money relates to your feelings and attitudes. For instance, do you spend more money on days when you feel depressed? When someone makes you angry, do you *get even*? If you;re mad at your partner do you"show him" by buying a new outfit?

See if you react to people by spending money, and if necessary, change the way you deal with stress so that it doesn't get in the way of your achieving financial success. Realize that you and your partner may have different attitudes about money. When you can begin to break out of the role you were choosing, you will be ready to follow your own personal budget.

"Budgets don't work because there are always emergencies and surprises." Really? Make a list of the emergencies and surprises in your financial history. How many of those surprises were really unplanned expenses? Look at your credit card receipts. Were these purchases rationalized as emergencies so that you would feel justified spending the money? Surprises are often birthdays, weddings, showers, taxes, insurance premiums and vacations. These aren't really surprises, are they? A personal budget will plan for these "surprises," and you can reserve money in an account, to pay for them when they are due.

What constitutes a real emergency? A ruptured appendix, car accident, heart attack, cancer, job loss—these are real emergencies. But are these emergencies really a surprise? Or are they a consequence of life style choices we make? If we change our lifestyle would some of these expensive emergencies be avoided?

The first year you use your personal budget is especially time consuming and crucial. That's when you'll be making changes in your spending patterns, but the financial rewards and peace of mind will be well worth your efforts. Is being financially successful a choice you are going to make?

*****

Why did you read this chapter?

_____

_____

_____

What is your resistance to the suggestions for change?

_____

_____

_____

What techniques have you chosen to initiate change?

_____

_____

_____

When are you going to start? _____

Chapter 16

WHAT TO DO IN THE MEANTIME

"And though hard be the task, keep a stiff upper lip"
-Phoebe Cary

*T*here are two reasons not to change, *fear and sickness*. Act on that knowledge and go on with life trying to achieve a balance among your work, family and personal life. Trying to live up to the expectations of the man or any other person in your life, is not being in charge of your life; and therefore not healthy.

Eight steps to meet your expectations of *you*.

1. Know that there is only one of you here today.

2. Review the chapters in this book that pertain to your life.

3. Prioritize and complete the chapter exercises in this book.

4. Document past conversations during periods of unpleasantness, so you will have responses ready.

5. Write and practice scripts to defend verbal attempts by
others to obstruct your progress.

6. Exclude the whiners in your life.

7. Develop relationships with women that are winners and in
charge of life.

8. Be a mentor to other women and encourage them to have
their own action plan.

*****

Chapter 17

WOMEN'S MOVEMENT

".....Remember all men would be tyrants if they could. If particular care and attention is not paid to the ladies we are determined to foment a rebellion, and will not hold ourselves bound by any laws in which we have no voice, or representation."
    -Abigail Adams letter to John Adams March 31, 1776

*I*n previous Virginia Slims Polls during the 1970s, the women most respected by American women were, for the most part, ones who had risen to prominence as the wives of famous husbands rather than through their own accomplishments. In 1990, of the four most respected women, only Barbara Bush - who tops the list - is prominent because of her husband. The other three - Oprah Winfrey, Margaret Thatcher, and Barbara Walters - all achieved recognition strictly through their own personal accomplishments. Do you remember Gloria Steinem's appeal to men for their support of the women's movement?, "You have nothing to lose but your coronaries!" On February 7, 1991, a report from <u>McCall's</u> magazine dated February 1991, stated, by age 65, women have heart attacks at the same rate as men. Remember the four Cs of hardiness and stress. (See Chapter 3, Stress)

Women and men think alike—both say men's behavior needs to change. For this reason alone, the outlook for solutions to the work and family dilemma is optimistic. Completing the "stalled revolution" is at least partly a matter of men moving from good intentions to actions.

Intentions are as far as most men get. They would like to be judged by their intentions. It is a point of argument between men and women that doesn't get resolved. How do you deal with the man in your life that intended to help around the house but "ran out of time" ... or intended to attend the children's school activity but "had to work late" or intended to recommend you for the next promotion but "didn't think you were ready" ... etc. Women in many instances accept the intentions but they are staying angry because it never is resolved. The dilemma continues. Intentions are just that, intentions. Expect results and you will get results. Don't accept the excuses.

The workplace dominates the area that women think changes need to be made in the 1990s. The following is a list of areas where women believe changes are needed:

» The salaries women are paid compared with men
» The day-care options available to working mothers
» Women's opportunities for leadership positions in government
» Women's opportunities for leadership positions in business
» The kinds of jobs open to women
» The kinds of marriages women have
» Women's roles as mothers
» Women's roles as homemakers

Take some time and think through your feelings about the Women's Movement. Resolve the conflicts you have on the issues. Chose an issue that would make your life better and join a group or write a check so the issue gets resolved.

The dictionary defines feminism as, "a belief in according women equal status with men, politically, socially, and economically." In order to make changes, women say they need to solve the dilemma of anger they feel. Feminism and the Women's Movement is the perfect course to take.

Do you fear being called a feminist? You know it is not a dirty word. Granted, it is used by men and women to signify that you are a trouble maker. Jill Ruckelshaus, an American Government Official, told hundreds of National Women's Political Caucus delegates gathered for their 20 year anniversary celebration, "it wasn't easy being a feminist. If you were part of the women's movement 20 years ago, you got blamed for communism, the divorce rate, inflation, the speed limit and poor reading scores."

The male counterpart label is to be a member of the old boy's network. Isn't it interesting that many men are proud to be a member. Why aren't we women proud to be a feminist and a member of the Women's Movement? "One is not born a woman, one becomes one." Second Sex (Le Deuxieme Sex)

An issue that has caused a diversion in the women's movement is abortion. Reflect on how the issue of abortion has divided women into two camps. Has there been an attempt to divide and conquer? We are now fighting against each other over this issue. Who's idea was it to divide us? Carolyn Heilbrun says, "When a women composes her own life, unconsciously or accidentally, she is considered eccentric, radical, unfeminine or odd. It is never considered to be part of the quest like a man's life, not goal and purposeful like a man's, but accidental ... after suicide ... broken marriage ... children raised ... not sexually attractive."

Carolyn Heilbrun also tells us in her book, <u>Writing a Woman's Life</u>, that women should share private and painful experiences with other women so we can know the real world and how to describe the real world in language women understand ... and how to express rage and anger and work through the periods of unpleasantness of the real world ... get a true descriptions of the real world for women ... don't worry about being confessional ... don't use the male model of distance and apparent disinterest ... Also in this book, Debrorah Cameron perceives that "men trivialize the talk of women not because they are afraid of any such talk, but to make women themselves downgrade it." Women's talk will indeed be harmless as long as women consider it trivial compared to talk with men. Jane McCabe tells us that "through anger, the truth looks simple."

The American Poet/Educator, Adrienne Rich wrote: "I think, women have a mission to survive ... and to be whole people. I believe that this can save the world, but I don't think that women have a mission to clean up after men's messes. I think we have to save the world by doing it for ourselves—for all women."

*****

Why did you read this chapter?

_____

_____

_____

What is your resistance to the Women's Movement?

_____

_____

_____

Which issue are you going to support?

_____

_____

_____

When are you going to start? _____

Chapter 18

WINNER OR WHINER?

"All pain is personal. It is between you and the thing that hurts. You may not be able to move the thing ... but you are movable."

-Charlotte Perkins Gilman

What is the loving thing to do? Take care of yourself and get in charge of your life. If you don't, you will not be able to be a good spouse, mother, career person, daughter, daughter-in-law, mother-in-law, sister, sister-in-law, aunt, grandmother, friend, neighbor, step-parent, etc.

The only ones wanting to be with angry and resentful people are other angry and resentful people or victims or chronically sick people. Why? Because they are not doing anything to make their life better. They are choosing to be victims and blame other people, places and things for their fate.

The Virginia Slims Opinion Poll, a 20-year perspective of Women's Issues, is an opportunity to look at what is happen-

ing to women's lives and do a personal inventory of your life
and change what is not wellness for you.

*****

Who are the *whiners* in your life?

_____

_____

_____

Who are the *winners* in your life?

_____

_____

_____

What techniques have you chosen to initiate change that will
eliminate whiners from your life; and add winners to it?

_____

_____

_____

_____

When are you going to start? _____

CONCLUSION

Women are 53 percent of the American population. Women can make a difference. The Hill/Thomas hearing in 1991 illustrated that when 98 percent of the Senators in this country are male, it will not occur to them to consider the value of the female. Representatives in the Congress and Senate are 94 percent male.

What was the reason the all male panel reconsidered the value of the female? Was it the women politicians that marched down the street? Was it the thousands of phone calls from irate women. Was it the pounds of mail? (yes, that's right, they weigh the mail before the pay attention to it) Was it the anger, frustration and rage felt by the women for not being heard? Was it the message given to these males by their spouses, mothers, sisters, daughters, etc ... or; *all of the above* was the reason that the all male panel reconsidered.

In her campaign for the Democratic Nomination for US Senator in the Illinois primary, Carol Moseley-Braun said, "Our institutions have to reflect the people's concerns, not just the narrow interest of millionaires talking to each other."

According to the 1990 Virginia Slims Poll, many Americans aren't ready to select a woman to higher office. After the medieval charade of the Hill/Thomas hearing, it makes sense to elect women to the higher offices so that 53 percent of the American population can receive equal status socially, politically and economically.

Women can make a difference when they support politicians that represent and value their primary concerns.

What are some of the concerns for women? Older Women's League, Gateway Chapter St. Louis, Missouri, has compiled the following *Facts of Life* for Mature Women:

• Almost one of two marriages end in divorce, after which the woman's standard of living falls by 73 percent and the husband's standard of living rises by 46 percent.

• Women earn 68 cents for every one dollar men earn.

• Eleven out of 12 women outlive their husbands.

• Average age of widowhood is 56.

• Median income of elderly women (over 65) is $670, just 58 percent of elderly men.

• Eighty percent of women (65 plus) receive less than $13,000 annually.

• Social security income for women averages just $458 per month, just 76 percent of that of men.

• Almost four times more widows live in poverty than do wives of the same age.

• Half of the widows who are poor were not poor before their husband's death.

• Nearly 75 percent the elderly poor, aged (65 plus), our fastest growing population segment, are women.

Sources for the data on the *previous page* are available in the O.W.L. office:

Gateway Chapter, O. W. L. • Older Women's League
4533 Moonglow • St. Louis, MO 63128 • (314) 892-1255

*****

We women together, 53 percent of the population, can and should seek and win financial equity ... for ourselves, our daughters and our granddaughters.

Women can make a difference when they support politicians that represent and value their concerns. Women can make a difference when they write checks to politicians. Women are 53 percent of the American people and when they use the power of the vote, they will no longer be discriminated against in all areas of life.

"To gauge the power of a woman's candidacy, ask the next five people you meet who Ferraro is. Then ask which tall, pale male she ran with." (Linda Witt)

Every Good Wish!

Sandra Brunsmann

OTHER PRODUCTS & SERVICES

Sandra M. Brunsmann is available for half-day, full-day workshops and seminars.

Some of her most popular topics:

The Gentle Art of Self-Defense (©Suzette Haden Elgin)

Sexual Harassment

How to Live the Good Life-Money Issues

Time Management

Work Expectations

There's Only One Of Me Here Today

Please call her office for scheduling dates and fee structure.

Note: *Please see <u>next page</u> for:*

STRATEGIES FOR CHANGE audiocassette and video tape ordering information.

STRATEGIES FOR CHANGE
By Sandra M. Brunsmann

PLEASE SEND ME:

Qty.	Item#	Item	Price Each	Total Price
		AUDIOCASSETTES		
_____	R-113	Dilemma of Anger	$9.95	_____
_____	J-0531	Burnout	$9.95	
_____	M-0972	How to Live the Good Life- Budgeting/Money Issues	$9.95	_____
_____	S-0542	Sexual Harassment	$9.95	_____
_____	B-031	Procrastination and Time Management	$9.95	_____
		RECOVERY AND RELAPSE PREVENTION		
_____	R-0636	Managing Finances with or without Spouse in Recovery	$9.95	_____
		BOOKS		
_____	B-0001	There's Only One Of Me Here Today	$9.95	_____
_____	P-0216	Plan-B Planner Simple Blue-Print to Financial Success	$9.95	_____
		VIDEO TAPES		
_____	V-0450	How to Live the Good Life Personal Budget and Money Issues	$19.95	_____

TOTAL $ _____

* Add 10% Postage/Handling $ _____

Missouri Sales Tax .05725% $ _____

OVERALL TOTAL$ _____

<u>MAIL</u>:

<u>Check</u> or <u>Money Order</u> payable to: S. M. Brunsmann

Bill my: Visa _____ Mastercard _____

Card #_____

Expiration Date _____

Signature _____

Call: (314) 822- 7010/821- 4761 to order by phone

Qty.	Item#	Item	Price Each	Total Price

Missouri Sales Tax .05725% $ _____

Add $1.50 (Per Item) Shipping/Handling $ _____

<u>Overall Total</u> $ _____

Print Name_____

Address_____

City _____ **State** _____ **Zip** _____

Phone(_____) _____

S. M. Brunsmann
1462 Royal Springs Dr
St. Louis, MO 63122-7134 (USA)
(314) 822-7010

References and Bibliography

Adams, Abigail; Letter to John Adams, March 31, 1776

American Psychological Association's National Task Force on Depression, 1990

Andrus, Kathleen

Anthony, Susan Brownell (1820-1906) Am Suffragist, editor; founder of Women's Temperance Society of New York; The Revolution Newspaper, October 8, 1868

Antonovsky, Aaron

Bailey, Pearl (1918-1990) Hurry Up America, and Spit, 1976

Baum, Vickie (1888-1960) Aus/Am writer, scenarist; And Life Goes, 1932

Beauvoir, Simone de (1908-) Fr writer, feminist; The Second Sex, 1949-1950

Braun, Carol Mosley (1946-) Politician; St. Louis Post Dispatch, March 22, 1992

Briles, Judith, author, speaker; Faith and Savvy Too, Regal Books, 1988

Brothers, Joyce (1925-) Am Psychologist, journalist; "When Your Husband's Affection Cools," Good Housekeeping, May 1972

Bush, Barbara, Am First Lady: "Address at Wellesley College, June 1, 1991"

Cameron, Debrorah; Feminism and Linguistic Theory, London, Macmillan, 1985

Cary, Phoebe (1824-1871?) Am poet; Keep a Stiff Upper Lip,

Clark, Jane Illsley

Elgin, Suzette Haden, PhD; Staying Well with the Gentle Art of Verbal Self-Defense, Prentice Hall, 1990

Friday, Nancy (1937-) reporter, editor, freelance writer, author; Islands in the Sun and Each Day a New Beginning, Hazelden Foundation, 1982

Friedan, Betty Naomi (1921-) Am feminist; nee Goldstein, founder of National Organization for Women, (NOW); The Feminine Mystique, W, W. Horton, 1963

Gilmann, Charlotte Perkins (1860-1930) Am writer, poet, lecturer, social critic, publist; early writer

Hielbrun, Carolyn (1926-) Am educator, writer, social critic, nee Gold; psued, Amanda Cross; Writing a Woman's Life, W. W. Norton, 1988

Koubasa, Suzanne; "Test for hardiness: How much stress can you survive?" American Health, September, 1984, pp 251-7

Koubasa, Suzanne; Health, Stress and Coping, San Francisco, Jossey-Bass, 1979

Larson, Darlene Jenks

Lerner, Harriet Golghar, PhD; <u>The Dance of Anger</u>, Harper and Row, 1985

Lindbergh, Anne Morrow (1906-) Am writer, poet; <u>Gift From The Sea</u>, 1955

Maddi, Salvatori

Maxwell, Elsa (1883-1963) Am hostess, writer; <u>How To Do It</u>, Little, 1957

McCabe, Jane; <u>Writing: A Woman's Life</u>, W. W. Norton, 1988

National Women's Health Network, 1992

Phelps, Stanlee and Austin, Nancy

Piccard, Rev. Jeanette; "one-women show," by Roberta Nobleman

Reddy, Helen (1941-) Aus/Am poet, singer, songwriter; <u>I Am Woman</u>, 1972

Rich, Adrienne (1929-) Am poet, educator; <u>An American Triptych</u>, Chapel Hill: University of North Carolina Press, 1984

Rowley, Carlene; "bank teller with Royal Banks of Missouri," St. Louis, Missouri; <u>There's Only One Of Me Here Today</u>

Ruckelhaus, Jill (1937-) Am govt official, lecturer: nee Strickland; "National Women's Political Caucus," 1991

Scott, Evelyn (1893-1963) Am writer; <u>Escapade</u>, 1913

Spyri, Johanna (1827-1901); <u>Heidi</u>, Ch 23, 1885

Steinam, Gloria (1934-) Am writer, feminist, editor, founder of MS magazine; <u>A Feminist Dictionary</u>, Pandora Press, 1985

Theisen, Kathleen Casey

Truth, Sojourner (1797-1883), <u>Narrative of Sojourner</u>, 1825 and 1970

Tomlin, Lily (1936-) Am actress, comedienne

Virginia Slims Poll, 1990

Winfrey, Oprah (1954-) business tycoon, <u>Lady Home Journal</u>, May 1990

Witt, Linda; "COMMENT," <u>USA Today</u>, 1991

Wortitz, Janet T. Geringer, EdD; <u>Adult Children of Alcoholics</u>, Health Communications, Inc. 1983